ELIJAH
TRUSTING GOD

Study by Linda Moore Lewis
Commentary by Judson Edwards

Free downloadable Teaching Guide for this study available at
NextSunday.com/teachingguides

NextSunday Resources
6316 Peake Road
Macon, Georgia 31210-3960
1-800-747-3016
©2018 by NextSunday Resources
All rights reserved.

TABLE OF CONTENTS

Elijah: Trusting God

HOW TO USE THIS STUDY

NextSunday Resources Adult Bible Studies are designed to help adults study Scripture seriously within the context of the larger Christian tradition and, through that process, find their faith renewed, challenged, and strengthened. We study the Scriptures because we believe they affect our current lives in important ways. Each study contains the following three components:

Study Guide

Each study guide lesson is arranged in four movements:

Reflecting recalls a contemporary story, anecdote, example, or illustration to help us anticipate the session's relevance in our lives.

Studying is centered on giving the biblical material in-depth attention while often surrounding it with helpful insights from theology, ethics, church history, and other areas.

Understanding helps us find relevant connections between our lives and the biblical message.

What About Me? provides brief statements that help unite life issues with the meaning of the biblical text.

Commentary

Each study guide lesson is accompanied by an additional, in-depth commentary on the biblical material. Written by a different author than the study guide, each commentary gives the opportunity for learners to approach the Scripture text from a separate but complementary viewpoint.

Teaching Guide

In addition to the provided study guide and commentary, *NextSunday Resources* also provides a *free* downloadable teaching guide, available at NextSunday.com. Each teaching guide gives the teacher tools for focusing on the content of each study guide lesson through additional commentary and Bible background information. Through teacher helps and teaching options, each teaching guide also provides substance for variety and choice in the preparation of each lesson.

NextSunday
Resources

STUDY INTRODUCTION

As a college student, I attended a retreat that included a session on "Trust." The leader introduced the theme by asking us to choose a partner. The partners faced in the same direction, a few feet apart, one behind the other. At the leader's signal, the person in front, with eyes closed and arms folded, was to fall backward into the arms of his or her partner. The exercise quickly revealed who in the group had a high level of trust and who did not. Some allowed themselves to fall without hesitation. Others could not resist the temptation to look back. Some were unable to trust the person behind them and refused to participate.

The study of Elijah challenges us to explore what it means to trust God. Elijah's story reveals that a life of faithfulness is built on trust in God's care and guidance. When Israel needs a prophetic voice to confront the nation's religious infidelity, Elijah responds to God's call. His first lesson in trust comes when he has to depend on God to survive. His experience will help us examine our own response to economic hardship.

Elijah's greatest challenge comes when he stands alone against the prophets of Baal on Mount Carmel. His actions are bold and unconventional, but he is convinced that he follows God's will. Through this dramatic episode, we will ask ourselves how we can be certain that we follow God's guidance.

Immediately after his dramatic victory on Mount Carmel, Elijah experiences a time of spiritual discouragement. In the midst of his despair, he has a profound encounter with God. We will explore how we can trust God to meet us in our darkest moments and offer hope and renewal.

As Elijah's time on earth draws to an end, he prepares to pass the mantle of prophetic leadership and his legacy of faithful trust in God to his disciple, Elisha. As we study this final episode in Elijah's life, we will think about our personal spiritual legacies. Elijah's story reminds us that we can face each day with confidence because we know that our future rests in God's hands.

Let's get to know this intriguing Old Testament prophet who has much to teach us about trusting God in all circumstances.

1

TRUSTING GOD'S SUPPLY

1 Kings 17:1-24

Central Question

What does it mean to trust God in times of economic hardship?

Scripture

1 Kings 17:1-24 Now Elijah the Tishbite, of Tishbe in Gilead, said to Ahab, "As the LORD the God of Israel lives, before whom I stand, there shall be neither dew nor rain these years, except by my word." 2 The word of the LORD came to him, saying, 3 "Go from here and turn eastward, and hide yourself by the Wadi Cherith, which is east of the Jordan. 4 You shall drink from the wadi, and I have commanded the ravens to feed you there." 5 So he went and did according to the word of the LORD; he went and lived by the Wadi Cherith, which is east of the Jordan. 6 The ravens brought him bread and meat in the morning, and bread and meat in the evening; and he drank from the wadi. 7 But after a while the wadi dried up, because there was no rain in the land. 8 Then the word of the LORD came to him, saying, 9 "Go now to Zarephath, which belongs to Sidon, and live there; for I have commanded a widow there to feed you." 10 So he set out and went to Zarephath. When he came to the gate of the town, a widow was there gathering sticks; he called to her and said, "Bring me a little water in a vessel, so that I may drink." 11 As she was going to bring it, he called to her and said, "Bring me a morsel of bread in your hand." 12 But she said, "As the LORD your God lives, I have nothing baked, only a handful of meal in a jar, and a little oil in a jug; I am now gathering a couple of sticks, so that I may go home and prepare it for myself and my son, that we may eat it, and die." 13 Elijah said to her, "Do not be afraid; go and do as you have said; but first make me a little cake of it and bring it to me, and afterwards make something for yourself and your son. 14 For thus says the LORD the God of Israel: The jar of meal will not be emptied and the jug of oil will not fail until the day that the LORD sends rain on the earth." 15 She went and did as Elijah said, so that she as well as he and her household ate for many days. 16 The jar of meal was not emptied, neither did the jug of oil fail, according to the word of the LORD that he spoke by Elijah. 17 After this the son of the woman, the mistress of the house, became ill; his illness was so severe that there was no breath left in him. 18 She then said to Elijah, "What have you against me, O man of God? You have come to me to bring my sin to remembrance, and to cause the death of my son!" 19 But he said to her, "Give me your son." He took him from her bosom, carried him up into the upper chamber where he was lodging, and laid him on his own bed. 20 He cried out to the LORD, "O LORD my God, have you brought calamity even upon the widow with whom I am staying, by killing her son?" 21 Then he stretched himself upon the child three times, and cried out to the LORD, "O LORD my God, let this child's life come into him again." 22 The LORD listened to the voice of Elijah; the life of the child came into him again, and he revived. 23 Elijah took the child, brought him down from the upper chamber into the house, and gave him to his mother; then Elijah said, "See, your son is alive." 24 So the woman said to Elijah, "Now I know that you are a man of God, and that the word of the LORD in your mouth is truth."

Reflecting

Brad and Libby Birkey grew up in families that valued helping others. After marrying and working for several years in technology and education, they felt moved to change careers. In 2006, in spite of the skepticism of relatives, friends, and financial advisors, they put all their savings ($30,000) into opening So All May Eat (SAME) Café.

What made this venture so risky was that the Birkeys opened SAME as a not-for-profit restaurant. The menu lists no prices. Customers pay what they can. Those who can't pay are asked to help by mopping the floor or cleaning tables. No one is turned away; everyone is treated with dignity. Homeless people and business executives eat at adjoining tables. No one goes hungry.

The Birkeys believe that all people deserve to eat well. They also believe in the basic goodness of people, and trust that those who are able to pay will contribute what their food is worth and maybe a little extra. So far, it works. Even with the economic downturn, SAME Café is doing well. The Birkeys may never amass great wealth, but their needs are met, even as they meet the needs of others.

Elijah experienced situations that stretched his understanding of what it meant to trust God to supply his needs. His experiences challenge us to think about trusting God during times of economic hardship. How do we balance our needs against the greater needs of others around us? What does it mean to place our trust in God as the provider of all that we truly need? This study will help us formulate responses to these important questions.

Studying

In 1 Kings 17, Elijah appears before King Ahab at a time when Israel faces economic hardship and religious uncertainty. He emerges unexpectedly as God's messenger to a king and a people who are spiritually adrift.

The kings before Ahab had their ups and downs. The writer of 1–2 Kings evaluates each leader on the basis of whether he did good or evil in the sight of the Lord. Ahab is described as one of the worst of the worst, provoking God to more anger than any king before him.

God finds it offensive that Israel adopts the religious practices of its Canaanite neighbors who worship a variety of gods. These gods are thought to control every aspect of life, including the weather, crops, and fertility. In their effort to survive the harsh, arid climate, it's no wonder the Israelites try to cover their bases. Along with their worship of Yahweh, they also experiment with practices aimed at pleasing other gods who might have a hand in their survival.

One of the most prominent of the Canaanite gods is Baal, the god of rain and vegetation. With the influence of his wife, Jezebel, Ahab has actually built an altar to Baal in Samaria. God cannot ignore this

In the ancient world, drought was understood as a divine curse. When God is displeased, rain is withheld.

blatant act. Elijah, a stranger from the wilderness east of the Jordan River, bursts into Ahab's court with a frightening pronouncement. Drought conditions will devastate the land until the God of Israel—not Baal—sends rain (v. 1). Elijah's word directly challenges those who believe Baal controls the forces of nature. Only Yahweh, the God of Israel, has this power.

After his dramatic announcement, Elijah faces three experiences that test his confidence in God's ability to sustain life. These experiences also validate Elijah as a true "man of God" (v. 24) and set the stage for a later showdown with the prophets of Baal.

First, God sends Elijah into the wilderness (vv. 2-7). His only means of survival are the meager water supply of an almost-dry brook and food delivered by ravens. God does not promise Elijah abundance, but merely what he needs to live. The writer gives no hint of hesitation on Elijah's part. He simply follows God's

A wadi (v. 3) is similar to a creek bed that is dry much of the time, but fills with water during rainy seasons.

command. His needs are met as God has promised. Before long, however, the brook dries up completely, an indication that the drought Elijah predicted is now reality.

Next, God directs Elijah to the city of Zarephath in Phoenicia (vv. 8-16). Here, he is instructed to seek help from a poor widow, whom he first encounters as she makes preparations for a final meal for herself and her son. Her desper-

> This God who comes down on the side of life is a universal God, who offers life even to a distressed widow of an alien people, of Baal's people, in fact. (Nelson, 114)

ate plight indicates the drought's devastating effects, even in the heart of "Baal country." Elijah's request for the widow to feed him must have taken her by surprise. Could he not see that she had nothing to share? Elijah boldly promises that if the widow shares with him, her last bit of meal and oil will continue to sustain her and her son until the God of Israel sends rain. The widow does as she is told. Her generosity, working in tandem with Elijah's trust in God's care, results in enough food for herself, her son, and Elijah.

Finally, in verses 17-24, Elijah demonstrates God's power to heal and restore life (vv. 17-24). When the widow's son becomes ill and dies, she first blames Elijah for the misfortune. Elijah takes the boy in his arms and carries him to his own room. There, in private, he pours out his own frustration, accusing God of causing the boy's death. Without waiting for an answer, he liter-ally throws himself into complete trust in God's life-giving power, stretching himself over the boy three times. His prayer becomes a petition for healing. Life returns to the boy, and, in a complete reversal of her previous mistrust of Elijah, the grateful mother now praises him as a true "man of God" (v. 24).

Through these three experiences, Elijah moves from passively accepting God's care to declaring bold faith in God's ability to provide all that is necessary. Then, he acts without reservation in his role as God's life-giving agent. He demonstrates to himself and others that people can trust the God of Israel to supply what they need for any situation.

Understanding

Even though Elijah's first lesson on trusting God comes in soli-tude in the wilderness, perhaps his most profound lesson comes through his encounter with the widow of Zarephath. It seems strange that God directs Elijah to ask *her* for help. After all, God sent ravens to feed Elijah in the wilderness, so why not do the same now? But as the story unfolds, the message is clear. The widow, nearly dead from starvation herself, willingly gives what little she has. Because she is generous even with her meager supplies, everyone has enough. Elijah needed the experience of asking for help just as much as the widow needed the experience of giving. There are times to receive; there are times to give. God honors both. At the end of the story, when Elijah revives the widow's son, the relationship comes full circle. This time, it is the widow's turn to receive from Elijah. Difficult times teach us the value of relationships and interdependence.

In the wake of a reeling economy a few years ago, the number of people without homes, jobs, food, and hope increased dramatically. As the smoke cleared, stories emerged about people using what they had to help others. NBC Nightly News began a series of such stories. Called *Making a Difference*, the series featured people like the Birkeys, mentioned earlier, who did what they could to improve life for others. Rather than giving in to despair, many people found ways to bring hope and make a difference.

Difficult times can open our eyes, not only to a new awareness that God will supply what we need, but also to the reality that God can take the smallest gift and multiply it in ways that bless the one who gives and the one who receives.

> How have you experienced God's abundance during times of adversity?

Elijah models how times of hardship can teach us about ourselves and about the trustworthiness of God. We can trust God to meet our needs. When we open ourselves to giving and receiving from others, there is plenty for everyone.

What About Me?

• *We can trust God to supply all that we truly need.* Times of economic hardship force us to distinguish between "wants" and "needs." The ravens did not bring Elijah a three-course dinner! They provided what he needed to survive. Elijah patiently waited and gladly received what God supplied.

• *There is nothing wrong with asking for help.* Our culture values independence and self-sufficiency, making it difficult for us to reach out to others during times of need. Asking for help involves making ourselves vulnerable, and it opens the way for deeper, more meaningful relationships as we learn to receive as well as give.

• *Generosity is not measured by the amount we give but by our willingness to share what we have.* When we respond graciously and lovingly to the needs of others, those gifts are multiplied exponentially. Like the oil and meal that never ran out, acts of love always find ways to generate more acts of love.

• *When we entrust our lives to God, we can become channels for God's life-giving hope in the world.* Many people are facing situations that leave them with feelings of despair. Those grounded in God's love see opportunities to respond to the needs of others in ways that bring hope and healing.

Resources

Walter Brueggemann, *1 & 2 Kings*, Smyth & Helwys Bible Commentary (Macon GA: Smyth & Helwys, 2000).

Jared Jacang Maher, "SAME Café: The restaurant where you pay what you can," <http://www.westword.com/content/printVersion/1029856> (28 June 2009).

Richard Nelson, *First and Second Kings*, Interpretation (Louisville: John Knox, 1987).

TRUSTING
GOD'S SUPPLY
1 Kings 17:1-24

Elijah's Big Entrance

John Morris, the priest at Saint Luke's Episcopal Church in Chester, Vermont, writes about a memorable moment in an American literature class. His professor told the students about Emily Dickinson, the quiet, reclusive woman who led a calm, unassuming existence in Amherst, Massachusetts. Next, he talked about Walt Whitman, the wild man of American poetry whose energy, sensuality, and wide experiences were dramatically different from Emily Dickinson's. The professor then offered two facts: the Dickinson family occasionally went to the beach for picnics; Walt Whitman was fond of going to the beach, stripping off his clothes, and running in the sand while yelling his poetry into the wind. So, he asked, what if one day at the beach, just after Emily Dickinson had finished spreading her picnic blanket on the sand, a naked Walt Whitman suddenly flew over a sand dune and landed in the middle of the Dickinson picnic? Who would have spoken first? What would that person have said? What poems would each have written afterward? What a moment it would have been for American poetry! ("Smoothing the Path," *Christian Century* [22 November 2000] 1215)

Elijah is Walt Whitman landing on the beach: a wild, surprising character shouting his prophecy all over the wilderness and howling his message into the wind. He shocked far more people than were willing to listen. It would be hard to go on with business as usual or concentrate on your picnic after Elijah burst on the scene. Elijah is either crazy or on to something big—or both. He makes it clear that the world is not what it appears to be. Elijah does not see the powers that be as the true powers. He wants a dramatically different world. He talks about the creation of a world of righteousness, justice, and compassion, the kind of world poets dream and prophets promise.

Much of this story seems like a fairy tale—a wizard who stops the rain, birds bringing food, a flour tin that never runs out, a jar of oil that is always full, and a dead boy brought back to life—but at the heart of the peculiar events is the hope that God is bigger than the accepted powers.

Elijah's Quick Exit (1 Kgs 17:1-7)

With little introduction, Elijah arrives uninvited near the beginning of evil King Ahab's reign. Elijah comes out of nowhere. He has nothing to recommend him—no money or authority. He is a party crasher, unannounced and unexplained, there to provide Yahweh's challenge to the followers of Baal (1 Kgs 16:31-32). Elijah announces divine judgment on Ahab's infidelity in the form of a coming drought.

We can hear Elijah's prediction in two ways. This could be a curse from God, who withholds the rain. The Israelites never had enough water and always feared drought. Perhaps the drought is God's response to the people's worship of Baal, a fertility god, a rainmaker. Elijah insists that Yahweh is in control, not Baal.

The drought could also be a slap at Ahab. The king's job is to assure fertility—which requires rain. In the ancient world, royal responsibility for rain was like contemporary presidential responsibility for the economy. A good king produced good crops (Walter Brueggemann, *1 & 2 Kings*, Smyth & Helwys Bible Commentary [Macon GA: Smyth & Helwys, 2000] 209). Elijah predicts that Yahweh is about to ruin Ahab's reign. Ahab and Elijah are heading for a showdown, but for now Elijah makes a quick getaway.

God sends Elijah into the wilderness, away from normal life. "East of the Jordan" is beyond King Ahab's control. Elijah's power comes from his refusal to be part of Ahab's kingdom. God will provide water from a wadi (a stream that runs only when there is rainfall). Ravens will feed Elijah.

Elijah's obedience is impressive. He is at the mercy of God's peculiar promise that birds will bring his meals. How much food can a raven carry?

Elijah goes and camps out. Sure enough, ravens bring him breakfast and supper, and he drinks from a brook.

Then Elijah's prophecy turns out to be true. The water stops flowing—for Elijah as well as for all of Israel. The king is in trouble, but so is Elijah.

Elijah's Care for a Foreign Widow (1 Kgs 17:8-16)

God sends Elijah to Sidon, a territory outside Israel. God is at work beyond King Ahab's limits. It has to be significant that this Phoenician city is in the home territory of Queen Jezebel. This is Yahweh's counterpunch against the invasion of Jezebel into Israel (Brueggemann, 210). Elijah might wish for more directions.

Elijah goes to Zarephath. The widow is at "the gate of the town...gathering sticks" for a fire. The nameless widow is destitute. She does not have any extra food or water.

If Ahab were a worthy king, then he would ensure the care and protection of widows. A widow in their society was in a perilous position. Deuteronomy prescribes protections because widows, like orphans and aliens, lived on the edge of society (Deut 24:17-22).

Elijah asks only for a little water and a morsel of bread, but the widow does not have a cup or a biscuit to spare. She plans to eat one last meal and die.

Elijah responds, "Do not be afraid." "These words often mark the promise that everything is about to change. The mysterious stranger seems less than gallant when he suggests he eat first, but he promises that the poverty the widow has come to accept will soon end. God will keep meal in the jar and oil in the jug until the rain comes. The promise of meal and oil changes the widow's situation completely. Now there will be plenty.

She does as Elijah says, and it turns out as he predicted—daily food for her and her family. God has put an end to her desperate need.

The writer of 1 Kings has what seems like an amazing lack of curiosity. This story was told and retold many times, and yet the writer gives no explanation as to how it happened. God provides, and that is enough to know.

God's Life Giving Power (1 Kgs 17-24)

Later, the woman's son becomes sick. The sickness takes a turn for the worse, and "there was no breath left in him" (17:17). The writer avoids using the word "dead," but clearly indicates that this woman will now be alone—a terrible lot for a woman in these times. She is in a man's world and has no legal rights. The testimony of a woman is unacceptable in judicial proceedings. A woman without a man to represent her is particularly helpless and defenseless.

The widow is so angry that she accuses Elijah of causing her son's death. Elijah responds by taking control of the situation. He carries her son upstairs and lays him on the bed. Elijah is angry with God for not caring for the woman who is caring for him. He offers two prayers. First, he asks why God did this. Then Elijah prays for the life of the boy. Three times he stretches himself out on the boy, praying with all his might, "God, put breath back into this boy's body!" (Touching the dead boy defiles Elijah. He is now ceremonially unclean.)

The writer says the prayer is answered. The kind of question we might ask—wouldn't God have listened to the crying woman?—goes unanswered. The attention is on Elijah and his access to God's power of life over death. Again, the writer expresses no curiosity as to how this happened.

Elijah must have been overjoyed to return the child to his mother. It is interesting to imagine not only how the widow's life was changed, but also how her son's life was different than it would have been if he had never died.

The woman says to Elijah, "Now I see that you really are holy. You speak with the voice of God."

The miracle calls for our attention, but it serves as a sign that points to the miracle worker. The endless supply of oil and meal and the son's return to life led the first listeners to understand Elijah's importance. He is now a force that challenges the king. The widow is overjoyed with the prophet, but those in authority learn to hate him.

One Like Elijah

When Jesus asked his disciples, "Who do people say that I am?" one of the answers they gave was "Elijah" (Mk 8:27-28).

In Luke 7:11-17, Jesus raises the only son of the widow of Nain in a story similar to our passage about Elijah. The tale in Luke highlights that Jesus is the continuation of the powerful prophets of old. The praise of Jesus sounds like the widow's praise of Elijah: "They glorified God, saying, 'A great prophet has risen among us!'" (Lk 7:16).

When Jesus raised the daughter of Jairus (Mk 5:21-43), many probably thought of Elijah. Like Elijah, Jesus ministered not to the rich and powerful, but to the poor and needy. Jesus cared for those who had no power.

In the Gospels, the essence of faith is how we respond to the weak and oppressed—not how faultless we are in matters of religious doctrine. We are to follow Christ's example by acting with compassion for the hurting.

We are still tempted to believe that power lies with those seen as powerful, but God has a different perspective. Elijah's story is a call for the church to challenge the powers, to stand with the hungry, the sick, and the widows against the establishment.

God's Story

Reading this story of God's power leads us to a bigger story. When we read *Moby Dick*, we feel vaguely seasick. When we read *Tom Sawyer*, we go barefoot. When we read *Lord of the Flies*, we look at our neighbors suspiciously. When we read Elijah's story, we imagine a better world.

Jane Addams, founder of a justice movement in the early 1900s, said this of her work in inner-city Chicago: "Much of the insensibility and hardness of the world is due to the lack of imagination."

We read the Bible to imagine, to let loose our tight grip on the way things are and imagine how life can be in God's goodness.

The church is an imaginative community. Whether we live out our holy imagining quietly like Emily Dickinson or exuberantly like Walt Whitman, we give thanks for the surprises that await

God's imaginative people. We open ourselves to God's surprising possibilities. We remember that we can never predict when God will appear, what lies beyond the next curve, or who will come leaping over the sand dune.

In Ahab's unimaginative world, poor widows and their children face bleak prospects. In God's world, prophets work for justice.

In Ahab's unimaginative world, teachers have begun a new school year and some are already just trying to get to the next day. Any idealism about molding young minds has given way to a single-minded focus on survival. In God's world, teachers and students dream of a world in which we care for those who are desperate.

In Ahab's unimaginative world, rich people buy what they want and hoard most of the rest. In God's world, we find joy in sharing what we have with the needy.

In Ahab's unimaginative world, some await the upcoming football season. In God's world, people choose to go to church and imagine our lives in the power of God.

In Ahab's unimaginative world, people read the newspaper and try not to take the news personally. In God's world, we read the stories of God's people and imagine a brave new world.

Imagine yourself as a subject not of the powers that be, but of the power of God.

Notes

Notes

2

TRUSTING GOD'S DIRECTION

1 Kings 18:1, 17-40

Central Question

How do I know that I am doing God's will?

Scripture

1 Kings 18:1, 17-40 After many days the word of the LORD came to Elijah, in the third year of the drought, saying, "Go, present yourself to Ahab; I will send rain on the earth." ... 17 When Ahab saw Elijah, Ahab said to him, "Is it you, you troubler of Israel?" 18 He answered, "I have not troubled Israel; but you have, and your father's house, because you have forsaken the commandments of the LORD and followed the Baals. 19 Now therefore have all Israel assemble for me at Mount Carmel, with the four hundred fifty prophets of Baal and the four hundred prophets of Asherah, who eat at Jezebel's table." 20 So Ahab sent to all the Israelites, and assembled the prophets at Mount Carmel. 21 Elijah then came near to all the people, and said, "How long will you go limping with two different opinions? If the LORD is God, follow him; but if Baal, then follow him." The people did not answer him a word. 22 Then Elijah said to the people, "I, even I only, am left a prophet of the LORD; but Baal's prophets number four hundred fifty. 23 Let two bulls be given to us; let them choose one bull for themselves, cut it in pieces, and lay it on the wood, but put no fire to it; I will prepare the other bull and lay it on the wood, but put no fire to it. 24 Then you call on the name of your god and I will call on the name of the LORD; the god who answers by fire is indeed God." All the people answered,

"Well spoken!" 25 Then Elijah said to the prophets of Baal, "Choose for yourselves one bull and prepare it first, for you are many; then call on the name of your god, but put no fire to it." 26 So they took the bull that was given them, prepared it, and called on the name of Baal from morning until noon, crying, "O Baal, answer us!" But there was no voice, and no answer. They limped about the altar that they had made. 27 At noon Elijah mocked them, saying, "Cry aloud! Surely he is a god; either he is meditating, or he has wandered away, or he is on a journey, or perhaps he is asleep and must be awakened." 28 Then they cried aloud and, as was their custom, they cut themselves with swords and lances until the blood gushed out over them. 29 As midday passed, they raved on until the time of the offering of the oblation, but there was no voice, no answer, and no response. 30 Then Elijah said to all the people, "Come closer to me"; and all the people came closer to him. First he repaired the altar of the LORD that had been thrown down; 31 Elijah took twelve stones, according to the number of the tribes of the sons of Jacob, to whom the word of the LORD came, saying, "Israel shall be your name"; 32 with the stones he built an altar in the name of the LORD. Then he made a trench around the altar, large enough to contain two measures of seed. 33 Next he put the wood in order, cut the bull in pieces, and laid it on the wood. He said, "Fill four jars with water and pour it on the burnt offering and on the wood." 34 Then he said, "Do it a second time"; and they did it a second time. Again he said, "Do it a third time"; and they did it a third time, 35 so that the water ran all around the altar, and filled the trench also with water. 36 At the time of the offering of the oblation, the prophet Elijah came near and said, "O LORD, God of Abraham, Isaac, and Israel, let it be known this day that you are God in Israel, that I am your servant, and that I have done all these things at your bidding. 37 Answer me, O LORD, answer me, so that this people may know that you, O LORD, are God, and that you have turned their hearts back." 38 Then the fire of the LORD fell and consumed the burnt offering, the wood, the stones, and the dust, and even licked up the water that was in the trench. 39 When all the people saw it, they fell on their faces and said, "The LORD indeed is God; the LORD indeed is God." 40 Elijah said to them, "Seize the prophets of Baal; do not let one of them escape." Then they seized them; and Elijah brought them down to the Wadi Kishon, and killed them there.

Reflecting

In May of 2009, pro-life vigilante David Roeder stormed into Reformation Lutheran Church in Wichita, Kansas, during morning worship. Before anyone knew what was happening, he shot and killed Dr. George Tiller, a member of the congregation who served as an usher that day. Because Dr. Tiller performed late-term abortions, Roeder was convinced that he killed the doctor in accordance with God's will.

History abounds with examples of people who have committed despicable acts under the guise of following God's direction. Certain that it was God's will to spread Christianity through whatever means necessary, Emperor Theodosius embarked on a crusade of death and destruction. Some Christians once believed that owning slaves was acceptable to God. Even today, discrimination based on race, gender, or sexual orientation is sometimes justified by the argument that it is God's will that we treat particular groups of people differently.

In contrast, consider the actions of Dr. Martin Luther King Jr. He believed God intended for all people to have equal rights and privileges. In response, he dedicated his life to addressing racial discrimination through peaceful means. The civil rights movement, which altered laws and transformed our understanding of race relations, was largely a result of his courage and his belief that his actions reflected the will of God.

As Christians, we profess a desire to live in accordance with God's will. We seek God's guidance when choosing a career, finding a spouse, and making crucial financial decisions. We pray for God to direct us to use our gifts and talents in ways that will make the world a better place. Yet, God's will often seems elusive. How can we distinguish between our desires, some of which are based on cultural expectations, and what God is guiding us to do?

Studying

For three years, Elijah managed to remain under the scope of King Ahab's radar. Drought and famine devastated the land, just as the prophet predicted. Perhaps Elijah spent this time in spiritual preparation, waiting patiently for God to reveal the next step.

Finally, God's word comes, directing Elijah to appear again before Ahab. This in itself is a test of Elijah's courage. The king blames Elijah for the drought and has placed him on the kingdom's "most wanted" list. This danger does not deter Elijah from following God's instructions, however. God promises to send rain to nourish the land, but first, Elijah must carry out an important mission to restore the nation's trust in God.

Elijah meets with Ahab and instructs him to call all the people together on Mount Carmel for a dramatic showdown between the God of Israel and the Canaanite god. Eager to be rid of Elijah and the trouble he has caused, Ahab goes along with the plan. The stage is set for a contest that will prove which god is most powerful. Ahab and the crowd are ready to see Elijah put in his place. He stands no chance against the huge contingent of Baal's prophets! But even though the odds are against him, Elijah remains confident in God's guidance.

As the crowd waits in anticipation, Elijah takes immediate charge. He boldly states the core issue: Israel cannot serve two gods. The people's attempt to follow the God of Israel and also dabble in the cultic practices of their Canaanite neighbors results in a life that "limps" along. They must make a choice: will they follow God or will they follow Baal? Suddenly, the people sense that these are not the words of a deranged fanatic.

> How does the indecisiveness of the Israelite people compare with the "lukewarm" faith of the Christians in Laodicea (Rev 3:15-16)?

Their silent and sober response to Elijah's ultimatum indicates that they have begun to grasp the spiritual significance of the day.

Elijah lays out the plan for the contest, careful to give his opposition every possible advantage. He is completely confident that Baal and his contingent of 450 prophets are no match for the God he serves.

The prophets of Baal choose their sacrifice and begin their appeal for fire to consume the altar. As Elijah expected, nothing happens. For hours, the prophets shout and pray. In desperation, their prayers heighten to a frenzy of dancing and self-mutilation, but to no avail. Could their god be asleep? Busy meditating? Away on vacation? Elijah's sarcastic comments paint the picture of a deity who in no way compares with the ever-present God of Israel who "neither slumbers nor sleeps" (Ps 121:4). The louder the frenzy grows, the more deafening the silence of their god becomes.

In stark contrast to the wild confusion, Elijah calmly asserts himself and takes control of the crowd. His demeanor reflects God's presence. As a symbol of God's desire to draw the people back into God's presence, Elijah invites the crowd to close in around him. Even the preparation of the altar becomes a sacred moment as Elijah uses twelve stones and twelve jugs of water to remind the people that they are descendents of the twelve sons of Jacob. They cannot escape their connection to God; they are who they are because of God's sacred covenant with their ancestors.

In an act of complete trust in God's power, Elijah insists that the altar be soaked in water, especially extravagant at a time of drought. Elijah is confident that God will send fire to consume the altar. He is also certain that God will keep the promise to send rain and bring an end to the drought.

With all the preparations in place, Elijah continues in an attitude of worship as he offers a prayer that affirms Yahweh as the God of Israel. Elijah prayerfully acknowledges that all of his actions on this extraordinary day came from God's word to him. Unlike the prophets of Baal who begged and pleaded with their god, Elijah simply asks God to do what it takes to turn the peoples' hearts around. Immediately, the altar bursts into flames. In answer to Elijah's prayer, the people profess their renewed faith in the God of Israel.

Some scholars suggest that the pouring of water was not to make burning more difficult, but rather was an ancient practice intended to produce rain during periods of drought (Snaith, 157).

Elijah's actions must have appeared strange and foolhardy. Yet, God's purpose was accomplished through his courageous commitment to risk everything and trust God's guidance.

Understanding

How can Elijah be so confident about God's leadership? We do not know what conversations Elijah had with God behind the scenes. Were his three years in hiding a time of soul-searching and spiritual discernment? As he confronted the prophets of Baal on Mount Carmel, did he quake inside? Did he wonder if he was doing the right thing?

We *do* know that Elijah was grounded in his trust that God's purpose would be accomplished. Furthermore, he made himself available to help fulfill that purpose. Unlike the people of Israel who "limped" along, dividing their energy between God and Baal, Elijah was wholeheartedly committed to God. With God as his foundation, Elijah faced each challenge trusting that God would work in and through him.

Hearing God's voice among all the other voices that clamor for our attention is not easy. Most of us experience God's direction as nebulous and elusive. We are pulled in many directions. Like the Israelites, our lives are fragmented by futile attempts to serve the many "gods" that demand our allegiance—the gods of money, power, recognition, pleasure, success. As a result, our lives "limp" and falter while we try to have it all.

> **?** What can Christians do to silence the inner "voices" that distract us from following God alone?

Perhaps Elijah teaches us that God's will is not an elusive plan "out there" for us to discover. Perhaps God's will is brought about when ordinary people like Elijah, and like us, become grounded in God.

What About Me?

• *Making ourselves available to God requires time set aside for spiritual discernment.* Life is busy. Full calendars and hectic lifestyles drain our spiritual energy. It is vital to be intentional about carving out times to listen to God's voice.

• *Being grounded in God means letting go of all other "gods."* A good way to determine which "gods" control our lives is to take stock of how we spend our time and how we use our financial resources. Are we using our time and money in ways that reflect our core values? If not, what do we need to change?

• *When we entrust our lives to God, we may find ourselves doing things that appear foolhardy and illogical to others.* God's work in the world sometimes calls for people who are willing to take risks and challenge cultural and even religious expectations. God's will is often expressed through the most unexpected circumstances and events.

• *We can count on God to give us courage when bold actions are needed.* When we commit ourselves to live in harmony with God, we may be called to take difficult stands against forces that work against God's purposes. We can trust God to make available whatever we need to fulfill our calling.

Resources

Marisol Bello, "Late-term abortion doctor killed at church," *USA Today* (31 May 2009) <http//www.usatoday.com/news/nation/2009-05-31-abortion-kansas_N.htm>.

Walter Brueggemann, *1 & 2 Kings*, Smyth & Helwys Bible Commentary (Macon GA: Smyth & Helwys, 2000).

Norman H. Snaith, "*I Kings*," The Interpreter's Bible, vol. 3, ed. George Arthur Buttrick (Nashville: Abingdon, 1954).

TRUSTING
GOD'S DIRECTION
1 Kings 18:1, 17-40

Standing Up for Truth

Martin Luther King Jr.'s father, grandfather, great-grandfather, brother, and uncle were all preachers. Martin grew up in the church, but he wrote, "It was a kind of inherited religion and I had never felt an experience of God in the way that you must if you're going to walk the lonely paths of life."

When he became the pastor of Dexter Avenue Baptist Church in Montgomery, Alabama, he still had not had a firsthand experience of God. Then Rosa Parks refused to go to the back of the bus, and Martin found himself in the middle of a boycott. Although he had only been in Montgomery for a year and was a mere twenty-seven years old, he quickly became a leader of the movement. It was not long before his family started getting threatening phone calls, sometimes as many as forty in a single day. He wondered if he could take it. He wanted out. Then one night, around midnight, another threatening call came: "We're tired of you, and if you aren't out of this town in three days, we're going to blow your brains out and blow up your house."

Dr. King described what happened next:

I sat there and thought about a beautiful little daughter who had just been born. She was the darling of my life. I'd come in night after night and see that little gentle smile. I sat at the kitchen table thinking about that little girl and thinking that she could be taken from me at any minute. And I got to the point that I couldn't take it any longer. I was weak. Something said to me, "You can't call on Daddy now. He's up in Atlanta a hundred and seventy-five miles away. You can't even call on Mama now. You've got to call on that power that can find a way out of no way." And I discovered then that religion had to become real to me, and I had to know God for myself. And I bowed my head over that cup of coffee. I will never forget it. I prayed a prayer, and I prayed out loud that night. And it seemed to me in that moment that I could hear a voice saying to me, "Martin Luther, stand up for righteousness. Stand up for justice. Stand up for truth. And I will be with you, even until the end of the world." I heard the voice of Jesus saying to fight on. (Drew Henson, *The Dream: Martin Luther King, Jr. and the Speech that Inspired a Nation* [New York: HarperCollins, 2003] 116–19)

That, of course, is just what he did. In all those years of going to church, singing in the choir, attending seminary, even as he served his first church—he had never heard the voice of God. Then, when the threat of violence began and he was about to give up, God came to him as he sat at the kitchen table. He heard a dangerous voice calling him to stand up for truth.

Two thousand eight hundred years earlier, Elijah heard the same dangerous voice telling him to call God's people to stand up for truth.

Elijah Picks a Fight (1 Kgs 18:1-16)

Elijah's confrontation with the priests of Baal on Mount Carmel is one of the most dramatic stories in the Hebrew Bible. The drought enters its third year, and the question for the Israelites is "Which God will provide much-needed rain for the fields and flocks?"

God commands Elijah to announce to evil King Ahab that Yahweh is about to send rain. Issuing this challenge takes great courage. It is a hard time to be a prophet.

Ahab is desperate for food for his horses and mules, so he orders the secretly devout Obadiah (not from the Old Testament book of Obadiah) to help him search for places where grass grows. Obadiah has already lived up to his name, which means "Servant of Yahweh." When Jezebel went through one of her "prophetic cleansings" (Terence Fretheim, *First and Second Kings* [Louisville: Westminster/John Knox, 1999] 103), Obadiah hid a hundred of God's prophets in caves and supplied them with food and water.

Ahab goes one direction and Obadiah the other. As Obadiah makes his way, Elijah shows up. Obadiah falls on his face and asks, "Is it you, my lord Elijah?"

Elijah wants Obadiah to tell King Ahab that he needs to talk to him. Obadiah anxiously tries to explain why Elijah should not ask him to do this. Obadiah is afraid Ahab will kill him if he passes along this message and then Elijah gets away. Ahab has teams of bounty hunters out looking for Elijah. In verses 9-14, Obadiah does not seem as committed as the writer says he is in verse 3. Obadiah begs Elijah not to put him at risk because he has shown that he is faithful to the cause of Yahweh's prophets. This odd interlude underscores the danger of being a prophet of God.

Elijah promises that he will not make a break for it, so Obadiah goes to tell Ahab. Obadiah then disappears from the story.

Game On (1 Kings 18:17-29)

When Ahab and Elijah meet, they immediately start talking trash. Ahab calls Elijah a "troublemaker"—one who brings disasters. Elijah courageously points out that Ahab has caused the problems by rejecting God and instituting the worship of Baal. (The plural "Baals" refers to local manifestations of Baal at different temples.)

Elijah calls for a contest between himself (and Yahweh) and the 450 prophets of Baal as well as 400 prophets of Asherah, a figure acting as something like Baal's wife. The prophets of Baal work for Queen Jezebel. Ahab appears to be "hen-pecked," completely under Jezebel's control. The king summons "all the Israelites" (18:20).

Elijah challenges the people to choose. Verses 24, 30, 37, and 39 make it clear that the Israelites are the reason that Elijah confronts the king. They cannot go on "limping with two different opinions" (18:21), sitting on the fence, and splitting their loyalties. Trying to serve two gods is rejecting the one God.

Elijah lays out the rules: "I'm the only prophet of God left in Israel; and there are 450 prophets of Baal. Let the Baal prophets bring two oxen. They can pick one and butcher it. I'll take the other one. Neither one of us will light the fire."

The challenge is to see which god will send fire upon the sacrifice. This may imply lightning, which is associated with the rain they need (Fretheim, 104).

The prophets of Baal take all morning. They go crazy—even to the point of cutting themselves. (In 1 Sam 19:18-24, King Saul falls into a similar "prophetic frenzy.") The prophets of Baal "limped about the altar" (v. 26). Nothing happens.

About noon, Elijah starts acting like a heckler at a comedy club. He tells them to yell louder. Baal must be asleep or taking a break or going to the bathroom. The prophets of Baal do everything they can think of, but there is not so much as a whisper.

Elijah's Winning Turn (1 Kgs 18:30-40)

Then the prophet takes center stage. Elijah calls the people closer and prepares a sacrifice that is fitting for Yahweh. Twelve stones represent the twelve tribes of Israel.

Elijah digs a trench around the sacrifice. In the midst of a drought, he soaks the altar and fills the ditch. Elijah is a showman making the trick more impressive. Three times he sabotages his chance of success by dowsing the altar with buckets full of water.

Elijah knows that God has promised to send rain (18:1). He prays, "God of Abraham, Isaac, and Israel, make it clear that you are God."

Suddenly the "fire of the LORD" (a booming lightning bolt often associated with Baal but also with Yahweh, as in Exod 19:18) consumes everything, including the water.

Elijah's success is seen in the way the people do not praise him, but instead praise God. The people respond by confessing that Yahweh is God.

Elijah boldly stood before the king, spoke his convictions, orchestrated the sacrificial act, and prayed with a sense of sacred history. This great story would be even better if we could skip verse 40, where Elijah commands the capture of Baal's prophets and then kills them all in a nearby stream. (Deut 13:1-5 calls for the execution of false prophets.)

We cannot explain away the violence, but we do not have to believe it is right. God deals with human beings as they are, with all of their faults. God works with imperfect people who misunderstand and make mistakes.

The story is clearly about God's power, but that may not be the central truth for the writer. The problem with Baal is that he does not listen: "there was no voice and no answer" (18:26). The writer is not simply saying that Yahweh alone is God. The story is meant to reveal the character of God. Yahweh is the one who "listens, speaks, and acts, and who honors commitments" (Fretheim, 105). This kind of God is the only God for Israel. This kind of God is the only God for any of us.

Choosing God

The contemporary question for many is not whether they choose the true God from the many gods, but whether they believe in God at all. Most of us in the church would say, "Yes, of course we believe in God," but the idea that we are claimed by a God who demands our complete allegiance in every part of our lives is hard to take seriously. We do not defiantly choose Baal, but we vaguely drift away to our own concerns.

William Sloane Coffin, longtime pastor of Riverside Church in New York, suggested the first commandment for Americans should not be "You shall have no other gods before me," but instead, "You shall have at least one God."

The common mistake is not worshiping any God. Many of us live without a sense of anything bigger than we are, because a thousand small things get in the way. We do not deny God; we just lose interest.

We live in a secularized and in many ways godless world, and yet we still have a longing, and a hunger for meaning. We have known moments of grace, often uncalled for and inexplicable, that belong to the mystery of God.

If we listened as intently as Elijah, we might hear God inviting us to find God's presence at the center of our souls. God's power will shape our lives and make demands. God knows our potential and recognizes how tragic it is if we invest ourselves in anything less than the divine.

If we listen, we might hear the echoes of Jesus saying that the greatest commandment is, "Love God with all your heart, soul, and mind." When we love God, life becomes less random and more focused, less confused and more meaningful.

I was not paying enough attention to catch the name of the conductor, but a commentator on a classical music broadcast described an orchestra's conductor by saying that he "devoted his life to the direction of his orchestra with a single-minded dedication that went out of style decades ago." That commentator may be right. Perhaps single-minded dedication is out of style, but it is a pity if it is so. We still have the possibility of a fulfilling, focusing devotion to God.

What would happen if we picked God over all other possibilities? Choosing God would mean experiencing God "in the way that you must if you're going to walk the lonely paths of life"; getting off the fence; challenging the authorities; standing up for truth; acting with courage; speaking our convictions; praying to the God of Abraham, Isaac, and Jacob; discovering that God is listening.

Notes

Notes

3

TRUSTING GOD'S VOICE

1 Kings 19:1-17

Central Question

Where do I turn for spiritual renewal?

Scripture

1 Kings 19:1-17 Ahab told Jezebel all that Elijah had done, and how he had killed all the prophets with the sword. 2 Then Jezebel sent a messenger to Elijah, saying, "So may the gods do to me, and more also, if I do not make your life like the life of one of them by this time tomorrow." 3 Then he was afraid; he got up and fled for his life, and came to Beer-sheba, which belongs to Judah; he left his servant there. 4 But he himself went a day's journey into the wilderness, and came and sat down under a solitary broom tree. He asked that he might die: "It is enough; now, O LORD, take away my life, for I am no better than my ancestors." 5 Then he lay down under the broom tree and fell asleep. Suddenly an angel touched him and said to him, "Get up and eat." 6 He looked, and there at his head was a cake baked on hot stones, and a jar of water. He ate and drank, and lay down again. 7 The angel of the LORD came a second time, touched him, and said, "Get up and eat, otherwise the journey will be too much for you." 8 He got up, and ate and drank; then he went in the strength of that food forty days and forty nights to Horeb the mount of God. 9 At that place he came to a cave, and spent the night there. Then the word of the LORD came to him, saying, "What are you doing here, Elijah?" 10 He answered, "I have been very zealous for the LORD, the God of hosts; for the Israelites have forsaken your covenant, thrown down your altars, and killed your prophets with the sword. I alone am left, and they are seeking my life, to take it away." 11 He said, "Go out and stand on the mountain before the LORD, for the LORD is about to pass by." Now there was a great wind, so strong that it was splitting mountains and breaking rocks in pieces before the LORD, but the LORD was not in the wind; and after the wind an earthquake, but the LORD was not in the earthquake; 12 and after the earthquake a fire, but the LORD was not in the fire; and after the fire a sound of sheer silence. 13 When Elijah heard it, he wrapped his face in his mantle and went out and stood at the entrance of the cave. Then there came a voice to him that said, "What are you doing here, Elijah?" 14 He answered, "I have been very zealous for the LORD, the God of hosts; for the Israelites have forsaken your covenant, thrown down your altars, and killed your prophets with the sword. I alone am left, and they are seeking my life, to take it away." 15 Then the LORD said to him, "Go, return on your way to the wilderness of Damascus; when you arrive, you shall anoint Hazael as king over Aram. 16 Also you shall anoint Jehu son of Nimshi as king over Israel; and you shall anoint Elisha son of Shaphat of Abel-meholah as prophet in your place. 17 Whoever escapes from the sword of Hazael, Jehu shall kill; and whoever escapes from the sword of Jehu, Elisha shall kill.

Reflecting

Barbara Brown Taylor spent nine years as a staff minister of a large Episcopal Church in Atlanta. Responding to God's call, she moved to Clarksville, Georgia, to become rector of a small church there. For five years, she devoted all her energy to parish ministry, earning praise as an outstanding preacher, a prolific writer, and compassionate pastor. As her notoriety grew, attendance at the little church increased. Every Sunday

the church overflowed with visitors who came to hear her preach. Gradually, the demands created by her success began to take their toll. The joy she once experienced in her ministry started to fade. In her memoir, *Leaving Church*, she describes her struggle: "I had done everything I knew how to do to draw as near to the heart of God as I could, only to find myself out of gas on a lonely road, filled with bitterness and self-pity" (123).

Life's demands can be physically and emotionally exhausting. Even doing "the Lord's work" can leave us fatigued and spiritually depleted. A schedule packed with church meetings, volunteer activities, and caring for others will eventually exhaust us.

In this lesson's text, Elijah reaches a place of physical and spiritual exhaustion. At his lowest point, he bemoans his situation and wonders why God has abandoned him. God's answer to his dilemma comes through a profound encounter that renews Elijah's spirit and reaffirms his calling.

Studying

Elijah's overwhelming victory over the prophets of Baal on Mount Carmel should have been an occasion for celebration. Any elation the prophet enjoyed, however, was short-lived. His decision to order a mass slaughter of the prophets of Baal enraged King Ahab's wife, Jezebel, who was instrumental in bringing Canaanite religion to Israel. No sooner had Elijah made his way down the mountain than he received word of Jezebel's plans to kill him.

Suddenly, God's messenger is on the run. He travels to Beersheba where he leaves his servant and proceeds alone into the wilderness, an area where Ahab and Jezebel have no authority. Here, in the middle of nowhere, he takes refuge from the

> Elijah knows that Jezebel's threat is real. According to 1 Kings 18:4, Jezebel had already commanded the killing of the prophets of Yahweh. Obadiah, the king's chamberlain, was an ardent follower of Yahweh. He secretly hid away a hundred of these prophets in caves and provided them with bread and water. Elijah was aware not only of the queen's murderous program but also of Obadiah's heroism in protecting the prophets (see 1 Kgs 18:13).

scorching sun under a small bush. Totally exhausted from the experience on Mount Carmel and from his desperate flight into the wilderness, he cries out to God in despair. "Lord, I can't take any more! Just let me die." With this prayer on his lips, he falls into the deep sleep of one who is completely exhausted.

Elijah is convinced that God has abandoned him. But he is about to learn that even in the midst of deepest despair, he cannot escape God's care. An angel wakes him, offers him food, and directs him to eat and drink. Too tired to protest, Elijah does as he is told and immediately goes back to sleep. A second time, the angel appears with a meal for him. Rest and physical nourishment renew Elijah's strength, enabling him to make a forty-day journey to Mount Horeb. Perhaps he hopes to get farther away from Jezebel. Perhaps he senses that he needs to make this journey for God to heal his spirit.

He arrives at Mount Horeb, finds a cave, and beds down for the night. Finally, he is ready for the inner spiritual work that must be done. God has provided what he needed for physical renewal; now God will provide what Elijah needs to renew his spirit. If he is expecting God to pull him from despair with words of comfort and assurance, however, he quickly learns otherwise.

> Mount Horeb is another name for Mount Sinai, where Moses met God and received the Law. Compare Elijah's experience with that of Moses in Exodus 33:17-23.

God confronts the prophet with a question: "Elijah, what in the world are you doing here?" (v. 9). God knows that instead of fulfilling his mission, Elijah is hiding in a cave. The question gets to the heart of Elijah's spiritual dilemma and unleashes a flood of anger and frustration. Elijah followed God's direction to take on the prophets of Baal, even risking his reputation by proposing a contest that could have ended in disaster. What is he doing here? He is feeling sorry for himself and wondering why God has forsaken him. It is obvious that Elijah is not where God needs him to be.

God does not respond to Elijah's self-pity. Instead he issues a command: "Go out and stand on the mountain..." (v. 11). Scripture indicates that Elijah does not follow God's direction

immediately. Perhaps he is being stubborn, or maybe he wonders if he really hears the voice of God. As he remains in the cave, a series of dramatic events transpires. In biblical literature, wind, earthquake, and fire are all associated with God's presence. Surely, this spectacular show is a sign that God is near! The text makes it clear, however, that God is not in these extraordinary events.

What stirs Elijah from his place of hiding is not the spectacular events that typically signal divine presence, but rather what Scripture describes as "a sound of sheer silence" (v. 12). In the space that is deeper than sound, when the voices in his head are finally still, Elijah senses a presence so profound that he hides his face. God comes to Elijah not in the extraordinary ways that he might have expected, but in sacred stillness. Moved by the experience, Elijah now emerges from the cave only to hear God's question repeated: "What are you doing here, Elijah?" (v. 13). Again, Elijah voices his honest complaint. He knows God is near, but he still struggles to understand.

This time, however, something has changed. Elijah, who was convinced that God had abandoned him, now hears God's voice clearly and distinctly, directing him to go back and finish the job he started. The sacred silence has awakened Elijah to God's presence and transformed his despair into a renewed sense of purpose. God reminds the prophet that he has a job to do. The nation's future depends on Elijah and the key role he is to play in selecting Israel's new leaders.

> God's therapy for prophetic burnout includes both the assignment of new tasks and the certain promise of a future that transcends the prophet's own success or lack of it. (Nelson, 129)

Understanding

Elijah's story illustrates the quick turns that life can take. In one day's time, Elijah transforms from a celebrity on a mountain to a fugitive on the run. Such quick turns are common in our time as well. Tabloid headlines that capture our attention in a supermarket checkout line often reveal stories of celebrities who fell from fortune and fame: the athlete who used steroids and got caught; the politician who confessed an affair; the movie star whose latest film bombed at the box office.

Those of us whose lives will never make the headlines can also relate to Elijah's experience. The job we thought was ours until retirement ends abruptly; the marriage meant to last forever falls apart; the good health we took for granted vanishes when a check-up reveals a major illness.

The journey from mountaintop to valley can be swift. Life can change direction in an instant. Like Elijah, we sometimes feel abandoned by God and resentful that we have tried our best, only to discover that life has disintegrated around us. At times such as this, the desire to retreat from life, and from God, is understandable. We want to get away from it all, hoping that we can escape our problems.

This lesson's text reminds us that we can go no place that separates us from God's care. Sometimes we experience God in the form of food and rest that renew us physically. Sometimes God confronts us with difficult questions that force us to evaluate where we are. And sometimes an incredible stillness enables us to hear God's voice and find renewed direction for our lives.

God followed Elijah into the wilderness, called him out of the cave of despair, and renewed his energy so that he could complete his story provides hope for all who face times of doubt and discouragement, times when we long to hear God's voice.

> **?** Can you recall a time of silent encounter with God?

What About Me?

• *Even people whose faith is strong sometimes feel separated from God.* Life presents many challenges. Our efforts to live in faithful obedience to God can result in spiritual exhaustion. When we feel that God has abandoned us, a time of retreat can allow for rest and spiritual healing.

• *God continues to care for us, even when we are spiritually adrift.* God's care may come in the form of physical sustenance and rest, or it may come as we are led to confront critical questions about ourselves. God is continually at work, even through times of doubt and discouragement.

• *Silence, a rarity in our noisy world, can provide the sacred space that allows us to hear God's voice.* It is sometimes necessary to find a space away from the cacophony of sounds that constantly bombard us so that we are able to experience the deep quiet of God's presence.

• *God meets us at our darkest moments and reminds us that we have a mission to fulfill.* Times of spiritual discouragement can force us to see ourselves in new ways and provide occasions for our most profound encounters with God. We can trust God to renew us by giving us new direction and restoring our sense of purpose.

Resources

Walter Brueggemann, *1 & 2 Kings*, Smyth & Helwys Bible Commentary (Macon GA: Smyth & Helwys, 2000).

M. Pierce Matheney Jr. and Roy L. Honeycutt Jr., "1–2 Kings," *The Broadman Bible Commentary*, vol. 3, ed. Clifton J. Allen (Nashville: Broadman, 1970).

Richard Nelson, *First and Second Kings*, Interpretation (Louisville: John Knox, 1987).

Barbara Brown Taylor, *Leaving Church: A Memoir of Faith* (San Francisco: Harper, 2006).

TRUSTING GOD'S VOICE
1 Kings 19:1-17

Elijah's Big Win (1 Kgs 18:17-40)

In the contest between Elijah and the prophets of Baal to see whose God is the real deal, Elijah wins overwhelmingly. Ahab, the king of Israel, must have secretly had mixed feelings. King Ahab has to deal with two pains in the neck. The first is the prophet Elijah. Frederick Buechner quips, "If a prophet is to a king what ants are to a picnic, Elijah is a swarm of bees." The other pain is Ahab's foreign-born wife, Jezebel, who got religion back in the old country and is forever trying to palm it off on the Israelites, who have a perfectly good religion of their own. Unfortunately, Ahab, Israel's worst king ever, keeps getting caught in the middle (*Peculiar Treasures* [San Francisco: Harper and Row, 1979] 9).

On Mount Carmel, the prophets of Baal pull out all the stops to get their candidate to set fire to the sacrificial offering. Nothing happens. Elijah gives Yahweh the word and jumps back just in time. Lightning flashes, and nothing remains but a pile of ashes and that burnt, post-Fourth of July smell. The onlookers are beside themselves with enthusiasm. You might think the euphoria from such an event would last for days, but it ends quickly.

Elijah Flees from Jezebel (1 Kgs 19:1-10)

Ahab reports to Jezebel everything that Elijah has done, including the massacre of her prophets. The daughter of Ethbaal, King of Tyre (16:31), and a Phoenician princess, Jezebel is not a worshiper of Yahweh. She vows to get even with Elijah for what he did to her crowd. She goes on the offensive, and the prophet is afraid.

Elijah runs for his life to Beersheba, which was often the starting point for journeys to the south, and leaves his servant there. Perhaps he wants to spare him the dangerous journey.

The people who saw Elijah on Mount Carmel likely found this flight hard to believe. Elijah's trust in God suffers a temporary lapse. This unflinching, unflappable prophet who fought for Yahweh and won chose to run away scared. This one who prophesied drought and watched enemy crops wither; who prayed for rain and witnessed a thunderstorm; who snatched a widow's boy from death; who stood before the king without fear; who confronted the priests of Baal and put their rain god to shame; who handed out miracles like they were going out of style is *frightened.*

Maybe the prophet's flight from Jezebel's vengeance is the result of a natural letdown after his triumph on Mount Carmel, but he does not seem like the courageous prophet of the previous chapter. Elijah's fear seems so out of place that some scholars think an earlier tradition of an appearance to Elijah at Mount Horeb was reworked to fit Elijah's conflict with the king (Volkmar Fritz, *1 & 2 Kings*, trans. Anselm Hagedorn [Minneapolis: Fortress, 2003] 196).

Elijah's Journey to Horeb (1 Kgs 19:4-8)

After only a day's trek into the Negeb wilderness beyond Ahab's borders, Elijah sits under the shade of a lone broom bush and cries, "I've had enough, God. Take my life." He wants to be done with it all.

Elijah took off in such a hurry that he has no provisions with him. God cares for him in a miraculous way yet again. First, the ravens fed him (17:2-7), and then the widow of Zarephath had a never-ending supply of food (17:8-16). Now a messenger of God brings angelic nourishment. The angel touches him and says, "Get up and eat."

How does God respond to Elijah's despair? God does not give Elijah a beatific vision. Instead, God gives him toast and a glass of water. "Elijah, have a bite to eat. You'll feel better."

Elijah eats and goes back to sleep. The angel comes a second time, shakes him, and says, "Get up and eat some more. You've got a long trip ahead of you."

Elijah's journey back to hope begins with a simple response to God's simple invitation: "Eat something because the journey is hard." For Christians, this invitation is reminiscent of the one extended at every Lord's Supper. Jesus offers this same hope to discouraged disciples. He knows we can't make it alone, so he gives us bread and a cup.

Elijah eats and drinks his fill, then sets out. Nourished by the meal, he walks forty days and nights, all the way to Horeb, the mountain of God. The forty days correspond to Moses' stay on Mount Sinai (Exod 34:28). The location of the mountain is unknown.

Elijah Meets God (1 Kgs 19:9-12)

Half-healed and unaware of what God is up to, Elijah finds a cave, crawls in to hide, and spends the night there. God does not leave him alone. Up to this moment, Elijah was too depressed and exhausted to hear God, but now he hears God ask, "What are you doing here, Elijah?"

Elijah feels like he is the only good one left. "God, it is you and me now. I've been working my heart out for you, and yet your people have abandoned your covenant, destroyed the sacred altars, and murdered your prophets. I am the only one still on your side, and they are trying to kill me."

The covenant was a binding agreement that obligated the Israelites to recognize Yahweh as the one true God. Israel broke the covenant by worshiping foreign gods. The altar was the only acceptable place for sacrifice, so reconciliation seemed next to impossible. Elijah's killing of the prophets emphasized the persecution of those who followed Yahweh.

In our passage, God reminds Elijah who is in charge. Rocks tumble down the mountain in a tremendous storm. A hurricane wind almost blows Elijah off his feet, but God is not in the wind. An earthquake almost knocks Elijah silly, but God is not in the earthquake. A fire threatens to consume, but God is not in the flames. Elijah expects God to speak through these elements, but there is not so much as a peep out of Yahweh. The traditional understanding of how God communicates is rejected.

Only when the fireworks are finished and a terrible hush falls over the mountain does Elijah hear something. What he hears is so much like silence that he knows it is God only through the ear of faith. In the Hebrew, God speaks in "a voice of gentle stillness." God whispers.

Elijah's Conversation with God (1 Kgs 19:13-18)

Elijah recognizes God's presence in a hardly audible murmur. This is a different image of God. The Israelites are not used to the idea that one can experience God in silence.

When Elijah hears the quiet voice, he covers his face and stands at the entrance of the cave. Silence asks again, "Elijah, what are you doing here?"

Elijah repeats his list of Israel's many transgressions. God listens to Elijah's complaints and fears, and then in the silence God cares for Elijah. Elijah hears God's still small voice of hope.

God gives Elijah a new mission. Elijah must go back through the desert to Damascus. He is to anoint Hazael as king over the Arameans, Jehu as king over Israel, and Elisha to succeed himself as a prophet. Many scholars see this verse as a prophecy after the fact (Fritz, 198). Elijah will not anoint Hazael. Instead, Hazaele wages war against Israel (2 Kings 9:14-15). A prophet sent by Elisha actually anoints Jehu (2 Kings 9:1-13). Finally, Elisha's call is reported without any mention of anointing (1 Kings 19:19-21).

There is no getting away from the coming violence. Jehu will kill anyone who escapes death by Hazael, and Elisha will kill anyone who escapes death by Jehu (19:17). God does promise to preserve the seven thousand who have not bowed to Baal or kissed his image. Seven thousand out of a population estimated at a quarter of a million seems small (Fritz, 199), but this is assurance that even in the face of a hard future, there is hope for those who trust in God. Elijah finds the courage to continue his ministry.

Strength for the Journey

Our lives are usually not as dramatic as Elijah's, but we know about despair and burnout. Have you ever felt tired without having worked hard? Do you ever feel like you need a break while you are on a break?

In William Saroyan's play *The Time of Your Life*, a woman asks the main character, "Why do you drink?"

Joe explains:

> Every day has twenty-four hours. Out of the twenty-four at least twenty-three and a half are dull, dead, boring, empty, and murderous. Minutes of the clock, not time of living, but spent in waiting. And the more you wait, the less there is to wait for. That goes on for days and weeks and months and years and the first thing you know all the years are dead. All the minutes are dead. You yourself are dead.

We can understand Joe's sentiment. A schoolteacher does not return her students' papers for two weeks. They sit in a pile on her desk, but she cannot muster the energy to look at them. An insurance adjuster listlessly prepares to go to work. He gets in his car and sits there for fifteen minutes unable to summon the will to turn the key. A teenager sits at home on Friday night staring at the television not because she has nowhere else to go, but because doing nothing seems easier. A church member sits through Sunday school without hearing much of anything. God promises strength for all who are weary, and we all get weary.

Who hasn't felt as alone as Elijah? Haven't you felt like you are the only person in the world with any common sense? Do you ever think you are the only one in your family who cares? That you are the only one who knows what the church should be doing?

Part of being discouraged is taking ourselves too seriously and failing to take God seriously enough. Remembering that God is with us means recognizing that we still have hope.

The high school senior is three weeks into the school year. For some, it is the beginning of another exhausting, drab year, but she takes genuine pride in her life. Unlike most of her fellow students, she is not fixated on competition. She is not trying to outdo anyone else. She is kind to everyone—even those who are not kind to her. She includes those who are not usually included. She makes high school more tolerable for those who find it especially difficult. Her life is an act of grace because she listens for God and does not forget that she is never alone.

When we are discouraged, it is often because we have put our trust in our own efforts, only to realize that we cannot make it alone. If we place our trust in God, we feel sadness in our failures, but we are not so discouraged. God is as loving after we fail as before we fail. Discouragement is evidence that we have placed too much confidence in ourselves and too little in God.

God asks us the same question God asked Elijah. When we are still, we hear God ask, "How are you doing? What are you missing? What can I do for you?"

The schoolteacher who cannot look at the papers on her desk, the insurance adjuster who cannot turn the ignition key, the teenager staring blankly at the television, and the one in Sunday school who is not paying attention can learn to listen to the silence.

God speaks to us, especially in our weariness. God invites us to share God's hope. In the simple response of listening, we accept God's gift of quiet hope. The journey is long. We need God's strength. We need to trust God's voice, even when it is barely audible.

Notes

Notes

4

TRUSTING GOD'S FUTURE

2 Kings 2:1-14

Central Question

What will my spiritual legacy be?

Scripture

2 Kings 2:1-14 Now when the Lord was about to take Elijah up to heaven by a whirlwind, Elijah and Elisha were on their way from Gilgal. 2 Elijah said to Elisha, "Stay here; for the LORD has sent me as far as Bethel." But Elisha said, "As the LORD lives, and as you yourself live, I will not leave you." So they went down to Bethel. 3 The company of prophets who were in Bethel came out to Elisha, and said to him, "Do you know that today the LORD will take your master away from you?" And he said, "Yes, I know; keep silent." 4 Elijah said to him, "Elisha, stay here; for the LORD has sent me to Jericho." But he said, "As the LORD lives, and as you yourself live, I will not leave you." So they came to Jericho. 5 The company of prophets who were at Jericho drew near to Elisha, and said to him, "Do you know that today the LORD will take your master away from you?" And he answered, "Yes, I know; be silent." 6 Then Elijah said to him, "Stay here; for the LORD has sent me to the Jordan." But he said, "As the LORD lives, and as you yourself live, I will not leave you." So the two of them went on. 7 Fifty men of the company of prophets also went, and stood at some distance from them, as they both were standing by the Jordan. 8 Then Elijah took his mantle and rolled it up, and struck the water; the water was parted to the one side and to the other, until the two of them crossed on dry ground. 9 When they had crossed, Elijah said to Elisha, "Tell me what I may do for you, before I am taken from you." Elisha said, "Please let me inherit a double share of your spirit." 10 He responded, "You have asked a hard thing; yet, if you see me as I am being taken from you, it will be granted you; if not, it will not." 11 As they continued walking and talking, a chariot of fire and horses of fire separated the two of them, and Elijah ascended in a whirlwind into heaven. 12 Elisha kept watching and crying out, "Father, father! The chariots of Israel and its horsemen!" But when he could no longer see him, he grasped his own clothes and tore them in two pieces. 13 He picked up the mantle of Elijah that had fallen from him, and went back and stood on the bank of the Jordan. 14 He took the mantle of Elijah that had fallen from him, and struck the water, saying, "Where is the LORD, the God of Elijah?" When he had struck the water, the water was parted to the one side and to the other, and Elisha went over.

Reflecting

When Eunice Kennedy Shriver died in August 2009, she was best remembered for her passionate efforts to improve the lives of people with disabilities. As an advocate for her own sister, Rosemary, and others who struggled with disabilities, Shriver worked tirelessly to open doors of opportunity and change attitudes. Believing that everyone deserves a chance to be a winner, she became the driving force behind the birth of the Special Olympics, an athletic competition for people with intellectual disabilities. The Special Olympics began in 1968 with 1,000 participants. More than forty years later, nearly three million athletes from 180 countries compete in the Special Olympics. What began as one woman's effort became a worldwide movement. An editorial appearing in the *Washington Post* soon after her death offered this tribute to Shriver: "Her legacy lives on in the millions of people she empowered to strive on the field of competition and beyond—and to be brave in the attempt" ("Eunice Kennedy Schriver").

> What are people likely to say about you after you're gone? What would you *hope* they would say?

All of us can name someone in our past who has made a significant difference in our lives—a parent, a teacher, a pastor—someone who influenced us so profoundly that their spirit continues to live within and through us. Likewise, we have an opportunity to leave our spiritual footprints on the lives of those who will follow us. How have special people touched your life and shaped your spiritual journey? What are you doing to leave a spiritual legacy for future generations? What can the story of Elijah and Elisha teach us about entrusting the future to God?

Studying

It is never easy to say goodbye, especially to someone who has shaped your life and taught you truths that really matter. So it was with Elisha as he faced the departure of his mentor, Elijah. This lesson's text tells the poignant story of their final journey together.

After Elijah's dramatic encounter with God on Mount Horeb, he follows God's direction and finds Elisha. As a sign of Elisha's appointment as his successor, Elijah throws his mantle over the young man's shoulders. Elisha leaves the field he is plowing and becomes Elijah's disciple (1 Kgs 19:19-21).

At first, Elisha remains in the background, soaking in the wisdom of the older prophet. Now, however, the time has come for Elijah to turn things over to his disciple. For both of them, the future is a vast unknown. Elijah must let go of his earthly existence and trust in God's eternal care. Elisha must take to heart all that he has learned and trust that he will be empowered to carry on as God's messenger.

From the beginning of 1 Kings 2, we know immediately that Elijah's departure will be extraordinary. It is not every day that God lifts people to heaven by a whirlwind! In preparation for his departure, Elijah embarks on a final journey, trusting God's guidance each step of the way. The exact purpose of the journey is not clear, but the underlying theme is the

> Elisha's loyalty to Elijah reminds us of Ruth's commitment to Naomi, to whom she said, "Where you go, I will go." (Ruth 1:15-17)

relationship between Elijah and Elisha and the awareness that their time together is running out. Three times, Elijah instructs Elisha to stay behind; each time Elisha insists on following. Is Elijah testing his disciple's loyalty? Does he feel compelled to face the end of his journey alone? Whatever the reason, it is clear that Elisha is not about to forsake his master. He is determined to savor every moment they have together.

At each stage of their journey, a "company of prophets" surrounds Elijah and Elisha and pulls Elisha aside. The prophets seem to know that the time for Elijah's departure is at hand, and they confront Elisha with a truth he already knows. Does he know that today is the day Elijah will be taken from him? Elisha's answer—"Yes, I know; keep [or be] silent" (vv. 3, 5)—suggests that there are no words to express the magnitude of what is about to take place. Some events are so sacred that the only adequate response is silence.

The meandering journey ends at the Jordan River. This time, the company of prophets stands at a distance as Elijah strikes the water with his mantle. The water parts, and Elijah and Elisha cross to the other side. They are now in the wilderness, away from all that is normal and civilized, ready for whatever God has in store for this time that encompasses both an ending as well as a new beginning.

Finally to themselves, Elijah and Elisha have an opportunity for an intimate conversation. It is not unusual for people who are near death to express a final wish—one last thing they would like to do, a loved one they long to see, favorite music they want to hear. Elijah, however, turns things

The final story, 2 Kgs 2:1-14, links the ministry of Elijah with that of Elisha, just as these two ministries had been linked in 1 Kgs 19:19-21. Elijah began to journey beyond the Jordan to be taken away by Yahweh and Elisha accompanied him. In every town they visited, Elijah instructed Elisha to stay, as he had instructed his young man to stay in Beersheba earlier (1 Kgs 19:3). Elisha, sensing the coming departure, dogged his master's steps. Finally, they crossed the Jordan together. Just before a chariot of fire carried Elijah away, Elijah asked Elisha what he desired. Elisha begged for a double portion of Elijah's spirit, which he indeed received because he saw Elijah depart. He also took Elijah's mantle, which fell to the ground as Elijah was taken, a mantle that seemed to possess magical powers. Then Elisha returned across the Jordan and went on his way. (Gregory, 244)

54 Lesson 4

around. He offers Elisha the chance to make one last request of *him*. Elisha is likely filled with emotion as he searches his mind for the one thing that will enable him to fill his master's footprints. He thinks about what an older son receives as an inheritance from his father. Elijah has become like a father to Elisha. Elisha does not request earthly possessions. Instead, he asks for a "double share" of Elijah's spirit. He may not be as gifted as Elijah, but if he has an extra portion of spiritual empowerment, he will have what he needs for the task.

Elijah knows that only God can grant Elisha's wish, and that much depends on Elisha's spiritual insight. He knows that the wish has been granted when Elisha is able to see his transport into heaven. First, the two who have become like father and son are separated by horses and a chariot that appear to be on fire. Then the whirlwind picks up Elijah and takes him up into the sky. Although his grief is enormous, Elisha must carry on the work of bringing God's message to Israel. He retrieves Elijah's fallen mantle, and with a mixture of hope and trepidation, he strikes the water before him. God does not let him down. The water parts. Elisha steps into the future, knowing that God is with him and that Elijah's legacy lives on.

> "Contrary to common portrayal in religious art, Elijah is not riding the chariot. The chariot functions, rather, not as transport but to separate the two, separating the one upon earth and the one in heaven, the one left with prophetic responsibility and the one taken up into the awesome realm of the divine" (Brueggemann, 297).

Understanding

Elijah vanished in a whirlwind, a reminder that life is fragile and the future is beyond our grasp. But as Elijah disappeared, Elisha was there to pick up his mantle. Elijah's life would continue to have meaning because the force of his faith lived on through Elisha.

How do you feel about the future? Do you look forward to it, or does the unknown fill you with anxiety? Life is uncertain. If you are a young adult, you may wonder how you will meet the challenge of parenthood or if you will succeed in your career. If you are middle-aged, you may worry about caring for your aging parents or what will happen if your company is downsized. As an older adult, you may be anxious about dwindling retirement savings or how you will deal with declining health and the loss of independence.

The future can indeed frighten us! We long for a path that is straight, clearly marked, and free from obstacles. In reality, we usually find that, like Elijah, we wind our way through a series of detours, never quite sure where we are headed. The poignant account of Elijah's final journey reminds us that our calling is to serve God to the best of our ability during the time we are given, trusting that God will lead us from one milestone to the next.

Elijah's relationship with Elisha compels us to see the big picture and embrace our connectedness to others—those who came before us and those who will follow. We wear the mantles passed on to us by parents, grandparents, mentors, and friends—people whose legacies live on through us. Similarly, one day we, too, will pass our mantle on to people whose lives we have touched, trusting that God's work continues from generation to generation.

> **?** Who are some of the people who have made a lasting impression on your life?

What About Me?

• *The future can seem overwhelming, but God will guide us one step at a time.* It is wise to make reasonable plans for the future, but we cannot anticipate all the turns our lives may take. We can, however, trust God to give us direction at every stage of the journey, allowing us to face each new challenge with confident assurance that we are not alone.

• *It is important to nurture relationships with the people whom God places in our lives.* We can learn from older family members and friends who have much wisdom to share. Similarly, we have opportunities to become mentors to those who are younger than we are.

Through these relationships, spiritual values are passed from one generation to the next.

• *We are not indispensable.* Life will go on without us. Letting go and passing the mantle to others creates an opportunity for us to share our legacy with the next generation. Have you taken the time to share your wisdom and experiences with someone who will be able to teach others as well (see 2 Tim 2:2)?

• *The future is in God's hands.* Nobody can see the big picture. Our calling is to live faithfully in the present moment, knowing that we can entrust the outcome to God. What present concerns do you need to hand over to God for safekeeping?

Resources

Walter Brueggemann, *1 & 2 Kings*, Smyth & Helwys Bible Commentary (Macon GA: Smyth & Helwys, 2000).

"Eunice Kennedy Shriver," *washingtonpost.com* (12 Aug 2009) <http://www.washingtonpost.com/wp-dyn/content/article/2009/08/11/AR2009081100917.html > (accessed 22 Aug 2009).

Russell I. Gregory, "Elijah," *Mercer Dictionary of the Bible*, ed. Watson E. Mills et al. (Macon GA: Mercer University Press, 1990).

M. Pierce Matheney Jr. and Roy L. Honeycutt Jr., "1–2 Kings," *The Broadman Bible Commentary*, vol. 3, ed. Clifton J. Allen (Nashville: Broadman, 1970).

Richard Nelson, *First and Second Kings*, Interpretation (Louisville: John Knox, 1987).

TRUSTING GOD'S FUTURE
2 Kings 2:1-14

What Do You Want?

David Owen addressed a topic that is too infrequently analyzed: "Your Three Wishes." He wrote:

> You have been granted three wishes—congratulations. If you wish wisely, your wishes may bring you great happiness. Before wishing, please take a moment to read the following frequently asked questions.
>
> 1. May I wish for absolutely anything? A wish, if it is to be granted, must not violate the physical laws of the universe. You may wish for Mount Everest to collapse into a heap of rubble, but you may not wish for the speed of light to be lowered to five miles an hour.
> 2. May I use one of my wishes to wish for more wishes? No.
> 3. How specific do I have to be? If I wish for "world peace," will you know what I'm talking about? As a practical matter, no one ever wishes for "world peace," but it is always best to be specific. "I wish to be a celebrity, but not Tom Cruise" is two wishes. (David Owen, "Your Three Wishes," *The New Yorker* [16 January 2006])

I write this commentary a few days after my birthday. My family asked, "What do you want?" The question is not as simple as it once was. When you are twenty-nine, you know what to ask for—a tennis racket, a midnight movie, a sports car. At forty-nine, the gifts are different. The problem with my tennis game is not my racket, I go to sleep around 10:00, and my 1998 Ford Escort gets good gas mileage.

I no longer know what I want. It took a while, but I finally came up with three wishes:

1. To have the leaves raked. This was also my Christmas gift. New leaves will be falling on the old leaves by the time you read this.
2. Six pairs of identical black dress socks. If you lose one, you're still in business.
3. Six pairs of white athletic socks with black stripes so that they can be identified when another member of my family borrows them.

I wished for an old man's gifts, because forty-nine is not young. People used to tell me I was young for my job. No one has said that in a long time. I am on my second pair of bifocals. I now have a tiny bald spot, barely visible to the naked eye.

I received a birthday card with a picture of a child jumping off a swing and a caption that read, "Was that your youth that just flew by?"

The older we get, the more we are supposed to know what we want, but it does not always work that way.

When we read the Bible, we hear the question, "What do you want?" At the Jordan River, Elijah asked Elisha, "What do you want?"

Elijah's Farewell Tour (2 Kgs 2:1-7)

Our story takes place eight hundred years before Christ. Israel is divided into two kingdoms with two rival rulers. Elijah is a revered yet controversial prophet. He has a long list of miracles under his belt, not the least of which is his recent success in a sacrificial altar-lighting contest with the prophets of Baal. He consistently earns Queen Jezebel's scorn. Elijah is a renegade. Oscar Wilde said a person "should always be a little improbable." Elijah is extremely improbable.

Elisha is Robin to Elijah's Batman, Tonto to his Lone Ranger. Elijah's final instructions from God included making Elisha his successor. Elisha has followed Elijah from the day the prophet found him plowing a field and threw his mantle, the symbol of a prophet, over Elisha's head. Elisha immediately left everything behind (1 Kgs 19:16-21). He watched Elijah with admiration, amazement, and a stubborn attachment.

The aging prophet knows it is about time for him to move on. He invites his young apprentice to go for a hike. They head to Gilgal in the hill country.

Elijah says, "Stay here. God is sending me on an errand to Bethel."

Elisha answers, "Not on your life. I'm not letting you out of my sight."

They go to Bethel together and drop by a hangout for prophets. (You will have to use your imagination as to what that might look like.) Some of the prophets whisper to Elisha, "You know that Elijah is going to be gone by the end of the day." Elisha responds with an anguished, "Yes, I know. Why don't you mind your own business?"

Elijah says, "I have to go to Jericho now. Do you want to stay here?"

Elisha answers, "Don't you understand? You are stuck with me."

They go to Jericho together and stop at the hot prophets' spot. More of them ask Elisha, "Did you know that Elijah is going to be gone by the end of the day?"

Elisha responds like an irritated teenager. "Have any of you ever had an original thought?"

Elijah is on a farewell tour of Israel's holy cities. He and his successor stroll down memory lane, except that memory lane is hot and dusty and filled with Elijah's fans. This tour is a round-about one. Elijah leads Elisha from Gilgal, near the Jordan, to Bethel, then back to Jericho (only a few miles from Gilgal) and the Jordan (Richard Nelson, *First and Second Kings*, Interpretation [Atlanta: John Knox, 1987] 158). Elisha patiently follows on what must have seemed like a poorly planned trip.

Maybe Elijah is trying to make it easier on his young friend when he says, "Why don't you stay here? I'm going to the Jordan."

But Elisha sticks to his hero like Ruth to Naomi, Butch to Sundance, Thelma to Louise. Elijah gives up on facing his future alone. The two of them walk to the river together.

Fifty of Elijah's admirers gawk from a respectful distance. Rudyard Kipling told a class of graduating seniors, "Someday you will meet someone who cares nothing for money, success, or fame. And then you will see how empty your own life is." When we meet someone as devoted to God as Elijah, we realize how empty many of our desires are.

Elijah Takes Off (2 Kgs 2:8-14)

The end is near. Elisha's heart is heavy. His stomach is turning. Elijah, who has a knack for such things, takes off his mantle—his preacher's robe—rolls it up, and hits the water with it. The river divides, and the two walk across on dry land, similar to those at the exodus and the conquest (Exod 14:21; Josh 3:17; 4:18).

When they reach the other side, Elijah says, "I've got to go now, but before I go, is there anything I can do for you? What do you want? Ask anything. It can't hurt to ask."

Elisha's voice shakes as he says, "I want a double portion of your spirit. I want your life repeated in mine. I want to be holy like you." By requesting a double share, Elisha asks for the inheritance of the eldest son (Deut 21:17). He wants to follow in the prophetic office of his "father."

Elijah responds, "That's hard. I can't be sure that is going to happen. God is in charge of gifts like that. But if you stay to the end and see when I am taken, I think you will get what you have asked for. But only if you keep watching."

Elijah makes it sound like this event may not be visible to the ordinary eye. Elisha's ability to see is being tested.

They are walking and talking when suddenly a chariot of fire and a team of flaming horses separate the two of them. Elijah is gone with the wind, taken in a whirlwind to heaven.

The burning buggy grabs our attention, but the writer is not as interested in Elijah's ascent as in Elisha's response. Elisha keeps watching and shouts, "My father, my father! The chariots of Israel, the cavalry of Israel!" It's as if he says, "Just for the record, I saw it all." When he can no longer see anything, Elisha sits down to cry. He rips his robe to pieces—an expression of grief.

Elisha is left with only the bundled wool of Elijah's mantle, the residue of the whirlwind, and the promise of a spirit. Elisha goes back to the shore of the Jordan and stands there.

He takes Elijah's mantle—a symbol of the prophet's office and all that remains of Elijah—and hits the river with it, saying, "Where is God, the God of Elijah?" When he strikes the water again, the river divides, and he walks through. The disciple can do what the master did.

It is not accidental or unimportant that Elijah and Elisha remind readers of the exodus. These are the liberators of Israel. They continue to do what Moses did, both to defy oppressive rulers and empower helpless people. If we are to speak of "miracles," then we must recognize that what defines a miracle is that it liberates (Walter Brueggeman, *2 Kings*, Knox Preaching Guides [Atlanta: John Knox, 1982] 11).

God transforms Elisha. He is a dependent protégé in verses 2, 4, and 6. He seems afraid of the future in verses 3 and 5. He is despondent at Elijah's disappearance. He still calls upon the "God of Elijah" in verse 14 and has to strike the water twice. But with Elijah gone, Elisha takes on the job of speaking God's difficult message to the kings of Israel. He has Elijah's spirit (2:15).

Choosing Wisely

James Cameron would love this pyrotechnic story: a phantasmagorical prophet; a river parting as if for Cecil B. DeMille; the original chariots of fire; Elijah's highly flammable exit. This story is so spectacular that we can easily miss a detail that is, in some ways, as surprising as anything else.

Elijah asked, "What do you want?" and Elisha, with all the possibilities he could imagine answered, "I want to be the kind of person you are. I want to give my life to God. I want to be a saint."

If you were asked, "What do you want?" a saintly spirit might not be the first thing to come to mind. We want this, that, and the other thing. We want a good job and a good home. We want to help others and to take it easy. We want to get in better shape and get the house in better shape. We want to read novels and learn Spanish. We want to do what we want to do.

When we are young, we want to be successful, rich, and famous. We dream of being rock stars and baseball heroes. When we get older and American Idol and the World Series seem unlikely, a hot cup of tea on the porch sounds nice.

We need to keep asking, "What do we want?" but we tend to avoid the question until something dramatic happens. When his teacher was about to die, Elisha thought about what he wanted out of life. We need to think frequently about what matters eternally.

What do we want? Do we want what Elisha wanted? Do we want genuine friendships? Do we want to live with God's Spirit? Do we want to visit holy places? Do we want to count ourselves among the prophets? Do we want to speak the truth? Do we want to give ourselves to God? Do we want to invest our lives in what will matter forever?

If we give ourselves to God, it will change what we want. We will long to be saints, to live holy lives. We will want to live simply, love generously, and serve faithfully. All that we could ever achieve is infinitely less than the hope of wanting more than anything else to give our lives to God.

Notes

Notes

nextsunday
STUDIES

1 Peter
Keep Hope Alive

This study of First Peter focuses on keeping hope alive in the face of pressures and circumstances that could possibly extinguish it completely, or worse, turn authentic faith into a pale replica of the real thing.

Advent Virtues

The phrase "holiday rush" is not an exaggeration. The frantic pace required to purchase gifts, bake holiday foods, and attend Christmas parties, plays, and performances takes its toll; we arrive at Christmas Day exhausted. Within the context of December busyness, the ancient Christian season of Advent takes on new meaning and acquires renewed importance. May God instill the virtues of *hope, peace, joy, love,* and *faith* in each of us this Advent.

Apocalyptic Literature

This study examines five apocalyptic texts in the Bible—from Zechariah, Daniel, Matthew, and Revelation. With each new year bringing a new prediction of impending doom, it is always a perfect time to get the story straight. Apocalyptic literature does not address the future. It addresses our present.

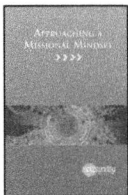

Approaching a Missional Mindset

The World isn't the same as it once was. We must be the church in a new place, in unimagined ways, and with a wider range of people. Engage your small group with the radical and refreshing challenge of developing a "missional lifestyle."

Baptist Freedom
Celebrating Our Baptist Heritage
What makes a Baptist a Baptist? Of course, the ultimate answer is simple: membership in a local Baptist church. But there are all kinds of Baptist churches! What are the spiritual and theological marks of a Baptist? What is the shape and the feel of Baptist Christianity?

The Bible and the Arts
God has used artistic expression throughout the centuries to convey truth, offer blessing, and urge believers to deeper faithfulness. In modern life, artistic expression flourishes, from movies to books to music to paintings to photographs. Sometimes artists are intentional about trying to portray God's truths. Other times, perhaps God is working even when the artist is unaware of it. As believers, we may hear and see God at work in many art forms.

The Birthday of a King
The first four lessons in this unit draw inspiration from a traditional interpretation of the Advent candles as the Prophets' Candle, the Bethlehem Candle, the Shepherds' Candle, and the Angels' Candle. The final lesson, which occurs after Advent, celebrates the theological meaning of Jesus' birth as described in the prologue to John's Gospel.

Challenges of the Christian Life
The way of the cross is difficult, and taking Jesus seriously means looking honestly at how we fall short of God's best hopes for us and seeing how much we need God's grace. For all of us there are times when we need to remember that Christ is our saving grace and recommit ourselves to the journey of faith, rediscovering, again and again, the life-giving purpose described in the book of Ephesians.

Christ Is Born!
Even in the midst of difficult circumstances, Advent is a time when we can find hope. Much like today, people in the 1st century church faced struggles. Examining the Gospel of Matthew, lessons include "Waiting for Christ," "Preparing for Christ," "Expecting Christ," "Announcing Christ," and "The Arrival of Christ."

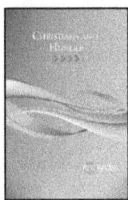

Christians and Hunger

These sessions challenge us to apply gospel lenses and holy imagination to what literally gives us energy to live: food. With God's grace, we have the opportunity to imagine communities where tables are large and all are fed.

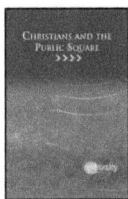

Christians and the Public Square

Politics and faith are tricky areas for Christians to negotiate. The First Amendment to the Constitution guarantees religious freedom for all Americans. As Christians who are also citizens, questions abound: How do we distinguish between faithful and unfaithful forms of civic engagement? How do we give Caesar his due while giving our all to God?

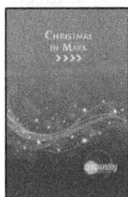

Christmas in Mark

In the early chapters of Mark, we will encounter a Christmas story. This story, however, will not be quite like the one told by other Gospel writers, but it will resonate with the reality of your life. Mark doesn't deny the beauty or reality of the nativity; however, he seems to believe that Christmas begins—the gospel begins—when Christ intrudes upon the hard realities of life.

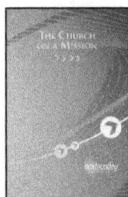

The Church on a Mission

What does it mean to be a church on a mission? The lesson of Acts 1:8 is that we must simultaneously carry out Christ's mandate at home, in our region, in places that have been our blind spots, and around the world.

Colossians
Living the Faith Faithfully

Paul's letter to the Colossians begins with a high-minded philosophical defense of the faith, but concludes with a collection of extremely practical advice for living by faith. This study addresses the questions many Christians face today, helping them apply Paul's practical advice in their own lives.

Easter Confessions

Easter confession is often found on many different lips in the Gospel of John. When we listen carefully, those ancient confessions still echo into this new millennium.

Embracing the Word of God

We live during a time of transition in Christian history. Basic assumptions about the truth of the Christian faith are being questioned, not only by nonbelievers, but by Christians themselves. First John offers a starting point for understanding of what it means to "be" Christian.

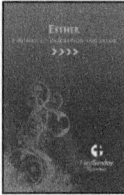

Esther: A Woman of Discretion and Valor

The book of Esther is not a record of historical facts as such. Rather, it is a magnificent narrative that refuses to interpret life as being driven by coincidence or happenstance. In the otherwise unknown characters of Esther, Haman, and Mordecai, we trace the movement of the divine hand as God collaborates with God's risk-taking people to rescue them from the hand of their enemies.

Facing Life's Challenges

This study explores four significant challenges common to most persons of faith: the challenge of new light, the challenge of time's limit, the challenge of living with mystery, and the challenge of authentic spirituality. Although these issues are neither simple nor easy to ponder, this study effectively leads us in confronting these challenges.

Forgiveness and Reconciliation

Forgiveness is a central issue in our capacity to remain redemptively connected to those relationships we prize. Restoring broken or interrupted relationships is a primary issue for all of us, and managing forgiveness is crucial to the possibility of experiencing reconciliation. Several dimensions of forgiveness affect our lives in significant ways. In this study, we attempt to address a few of those important issues.

The Four Cardinal Virtues

Christians are learning how to distinguish between members of a church and disciples of Christ. Discipleship involves developing virtues in those who come to our churches seeking life, salvation, grace, mercy. If we want to have something to offer a world in desperate need, then we must return to virtues like discernment, justice, courage, and moderation. We must return to the hard and glorious work of making disciples.

Galatians
Freedom in Christ

Paul wrote with fiery passion, as you will notice from the opening paragraphs of this letter to the Galatians. But his language reveals that he was writing about a crucially important issue—the very nature of salvation in Christ.

Godly Leadership

Nehemiah was called to return to Jerusalem to lead in the sacred task of rebuilding the city's walls. Displaying characteristics often lacking in secular leadership—prayerful humility, a willingness to work with diverse teams, wisdom in confronting conflict, and a passion to stand with the powerless—Nehemiah offered his people a portrait of godly leadership that can still shape our own calls to lead nearly 2,500 years later.

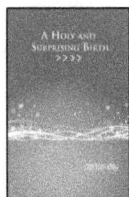

A Holy and Surprising Birth

Christmas begins here—discover these five love stories from the book of Luke and renew your appreciation of God's laborious effort to birth our salvation.

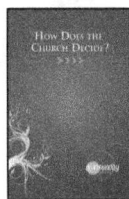

How Does the Church Decide?

An array of decisions draw energy and time from church members. These decisions may be theological, such as mode of baptism, aesthetic, such as the color of the sanctuary carpet, or functional, such as the selection of a new minister. This study will consider how the church has made its decisions in the past to help guide our decisions today.

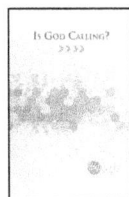

Is God Calling?

Witness the varying forms of God's call, the variety of people called, and the variety of responses. Perhaps God's call to you will become clearer.

James
Gaining True Wisdom
If we'll be honest with God and ourselves as we study what James says, we can make great strides toward wisdom and a living faith.

Life Lessons from Bathsheba
Who was Bathsheba? She was a complex figure who developed from the silent object of David's lust into a powerful, vocal, and influential queen mother.

Life Lessons from David
In the Bible, we catch David in the various stages of the human journey: childhood, adolescence, adulthood, and senior adulthood. From the biblical treatment of the stages of David's life, we can land some insights to assist us in better understanding the human journey.

The Matriarchs
The matriarchs of Genesis offer their lives as a testimony of faith, perseverance, and audacity. We learn from their mistakes and suffering. We will gain the hope of Hagar, the joy of Sarah, and the audacity of Rebekah as we are challenged to examine our prejudices and our insecurities while studying Esau and Jacob's wives.

Missional Hospitality
If we are serious about following Jesus, we will be people of open hearts, open hands, and open homes. In other words, as followers of Jesus we will practice the fine art of hospitality. In lesson one, we reflect on hospitality to strangers. In lesson two, we address hospitality to the poor. In lesson three, we focus on hospitality to sinners. In lesson four, we learn about hospitality to newcomers. Lesson five reminds us about our hospitality to Christ.

Moses
From the Burning Bush to the Promised Land
We would do well to trace the life of Moses so we might discover how his life changed, both personally and as Israel's leader, as he learned what it meant to love God with all his heart, soul, and strength.

Old Testament Promises to God

Some individuals may feel that our promises couldn't possibly mean anything to God. Perhaps the real question is this: under what circumstances should or do we make such promises? The Old Testament contains several examples of people making promises to God, using the unique form of a biblical "vow."

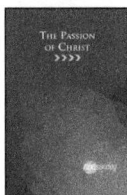

The Passion of Christ

The four lessons in this unit highlight the faith struggles of the early disciples. In lesson one, Jesus addresses the issues of faith and practice. In lesson two, we meet Judas who, like us, struggled with God's Kingdom and human kingdoms. In lesson three, the issue of temptation reminds us that our faith journey is a constant challenge. Lesson Four invites us to remember Peter's experience of "faith failure." Peter's failure, however, is not the final word. There is forgiveness.

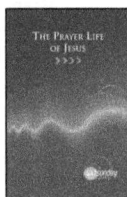

The Prayer Life of Jesus

The study of Jesus' prayer life can deepen our own prayer practices. These five sessions examine the importance of prayer at various stages of Jesus' life and ministry. He made no important decisions without consulting God.

Prepare the Way

In these sessions, we will seek to prepare the way toward and into the Christmas season. We begin with the theme of hopeful watchfulness in light of the coming of Christ. Next, we will spend two sessions considering the ministry of John the Baptist, the forerunner of Christ. Then, we will consider Matthew's account of the birth of Jesus and join in wonder at the miracle of "God with us." Finally, we will remember the story of the "holy innocents" killed by Herod in his attempt to eliminate the Christ child's threat to his power.

Proverbs for Living

Long ago, a collection of wise teachers committed themselves to the ways of God and collected this wisdom into what we know as the book of Proverbs. These four lessons explore the simple truth of Proverbs: there is a good life to be had—a life lived in faithfulness to God.

Qualities of Our Missional God

Too often we are tempted to let "numbers" drive missions. The book of Numbers reminds us that missions is motivated by something deeper. Missions reflects the heart and nature of God. If we can just get past the math, we can see God's nature clearly in the book of Numbers. . . in the wilderness.

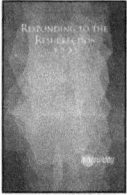

Responding to the Resurrection

All major events of human history elicit responses as varied as the personalities and situations represented by those affected. No one witnesses a world-changing event without being affected in some way. Studying the response of early followers helps us to shape our own response to the resurrection of Jesus. Each of us must consider our response to Jesus' life, teachings, death, resurrection, and call on our lives.

The Seven Deadly Sins

What exactly is sin? Just as we organize our cupboards and our schedules to make sense of our lives, Christian thinkers have organized sin into a number of categories in order to understand and surrender these patterns to God. The notion of "seven deadly sins" emerged as a way to recognize specific dangers to our spiritual lives. The purpose of the book is to guide people away from sin and into a wise and godly life.

Seeking Holiness in the Sermon on the Mount

The Sermon on the Mount has long been recognized as the pinnacle of Jesus' teaching. But with this importance in mind, it's easy to think of Jesus' teachings as lofty and idealistic, offering little guidance for everyday life. Perhaps Jesus' sermon allows us to see beyond ourselves, beyond our own failures and shortcomings— revealing God's intention for our lives.

Sing We Now of Christmas

In this study, we will explore some familiar prophecies, as well as the Gospel birth narratives, through the lens of five traditional Christmas carols. As carols have grown to be a fuller and more meaningful part of our worship and celebration, so too can the stories of Jesus' birth continue to grow within us and enrich our faith experience.

Spiritual Disciplines
Obligation or Opportunity?

The spiritual disciplines help deepen a believer's faith and increases his or her intimacy with Christ. In this study, we take a deeper look at some of the disciplines and consider their practice as a response to God's love.

Stewardship
A Way of Living

Great News! Stewardship is not about money! At least not *just* about money. Certainly, stewardship relates to money, and, yes, we need to tithe. However, stewardship branches out into multiple areas of life. Properly practiced, this act of service can lead to peace and purpose in living.

The Ten Commandments

When the Ten Commandments are in the news, it is usually because a judge or teacher has hung them up on the walls. The Ten Commandments do not need to be posted or even preached nearly so much as they need to be practiced and viewed as life-giving, joyful affirmations of a better way of life.

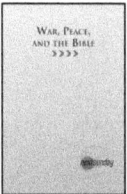

War, Peace, and the Bible

As people of faith, we are faced daily with an expectation that we participate in violent actions, our willingness to allow violence in the world to continue, and our response to violence in our lives. Is there a place for war and violence in our faith?

What Would Jesus Say?
A Lenten Study

To address what Jesus would say, we need to discover what Jesus did say. These lessons will attempt to help us understand Jesus' teachings and apply them today.

The Wonder of Easter

In 1 Corinthians 15, Paul asserts that the message that Jesus died for our sins, was buried, and rose on the third day is "of first importance" (v. 3). It is the core of the gospel story and of the Christian faith. But as much as Easter is a mystery to contemplate, it is also a hope to embrace and good news to proclaim.

**NextSunday Studies
are available from**

NextSunday
Resources

www.ingramcontent.com/pod-product-compliance
Lightning Source LLC
Chambersburg PA
CBHW060652030426
42337CB00017B/2571